La Llorona

Also known as "The Wailing Woman"

An ancient Mexican Legend adapted from the Spanish into
Middle-Modern American English
by

Yda Addis

First published 1888, in the San Francisco bi-weekly journal
The Argonaut

Introduction by Sterling Saint James
Translation from Middle-Modern English into Present-Day English by Sterling Saint James

Cover illustration by Nancy Glenn-Nieto

Copyright 2015 © S.S.J. Trust

All rights reserved. No part of this book may be reproduced or transmitted in any form or by any means, electronic or mechanical, including photocopying, recording, or by any information storage and retrieval system, without permission in writing from the publisher.

Published by Parhelion House

Parhelion House, Publisher
info@ParhelionHouse.com

ISBN-13: 978-0989369527
ISBN-10: 0989369528

Contents

Introduction 5

La Llorona 29

The Front Cover 41

Introduction

Although *La Llorona* is an ancient Mexican legend about an illicit sexual relationship, oddly the Church during the Mexican Inquisition most likely was responsible for the story's creation and dissemination. The reason for which was to contend with one of the greatest problems it faced during early Colonial Mexico and that was the Spanish conquistadores.

These men upon their arrival to Mexico felt no restraints or moral qualms about their sexual behavior. Even though some had taken the vow of Holy Matrimony and left their wives in Spain; in spite of this many were having illicit relationships with the women they met in the new land. Not only were the Conquistadores sinning, but the children born from these affairs could not be baptized.

The Conquerors were of the old military tradition. They were enchanted with danger, fighting, killing, and taking by force. They came to the new land to reap wealth from their actions, but received little more than the price of a horse.

Introduction

Disillusioned and disappointed, unrest among the military was widespread.

These men craved adventure; not colonization; even though they were devout in their religious observances confessing their sins, and praying frequently, especially before going into combat, they sought no religious sanctuary, nor were they interested in searching for and establishing fields to grow crops or to raise livestock. Their purpose for coming to the new land was to conquer, they were successful not only in war, but with women.

Illicit sexual relationships were not exclusive to the military. There were also problems with the secular clergymen. While the old world style of religious cloistered living gave way in Mexico to a more open life style, this situation led to opportunities. Even persons of high official positions were accused of moral offenses such as adultery, bigamy, and blasphemy. No matter if they were military, ecclesiastic, nobles, or politicians, when found culpable, all endured the same sentences. The guilty received floggings, fines, service in the galleys, or exile.

The relaxed morality in Mexico gave way to a new phenomenon for the Church and that was how to control the sexual behavior of powerful men, of conquerors, and even some of the clergy. To regain dominance the Church focused not upon the men, but on the women. The Church spread propaganda warning women that

> One whose life is pure lives in safety, but one whose ways are crooked is brought low." Proverbs 10:3:9

But reiterating Proverbs was not effective. Instead, the Church followed the wisdom of those who wrote the Bible. In Colonial Mexico the *La Llorona* parable was used to shock those who were drifting from its teachings.

The Inquisition tightly controlled the printing presses, and banned the publication of *La Llorona* on the grounds that it was sacrilegious and contrary to morality. Even the folksong that was based upon the legend never mentioned what La Llorona did only that it was a black endeavor. To shun the responsibility of acknowledging authorship of such a vile story, the tale of *La Llorona* survived for centuries passed down through the oral tradition. For that reason the legend developed different twists and variations.

However, in 1885 when the American writer Yda Addis visited friends in Mexico City she heard the story of the virginal young maiden's fall from grace at the seduction of a Spanish nobleman. Immediately Yda became intrigued because many of her stories had themes that dealt with the unleashing of morals. She herself had left the United States due to a romantic misunderstanding with the former California Governor John Downey.

Scandalous rumors spread after she had been seen publicly in San Francisco riding with the elder gentlemen in his carriage; questions arose as to her purpose: Why would an attractive young woman want to keep company with a man more than thirty years her senior?

Above: Governor John Downey as a young man.

When Downey's two younger sisters discovered that he had proposed marriage to such a youthful female, they believed she was a gold digger. If he were to marry, they would loose their places in line of inheritance. In order to protect their potential interest in his vast estate, they had him shanghaied, and taken to his native homeland Ireland.

With Downey's disappearance before the marriage, Yda was humiliated, and her reputation irrevocable dented. Her father demanded that she sue him for breach of promise; in that way the ex-Governor would be forced to come out of hiding to explain his actions. On the other hand, if Downey did not contest the case, she could win by default. Either way she would be financially justified for the damage Downey did to her reputation. As a jilted woman she would have few, perhaps no opportunities to wed within the high society of San Francisco.

At her father's strong disapproval, she refused to take the ex-Governor to court. In that way she was able to save her business relationship with Frank Pixley who had introduced the young authoress to Downey.

Pixley was the founder and publisher of the San Francisco based political and literary journal *The Argonaut*. He discovered the young writer when his friend and political crony Judge Ignacio Sepulveda of Los Angeles sent him her

Introduction

first story entitled *Doctor Craft's Mistake*. That was in 1880. By the time Yda met Downey in 1885 she had become a well known authoress due to Pixley's publication that regularly featured her newest stories. She was paid from $50.00 to $150.00 for each narrative depending on the length or number of words. Factoring for inflation, in 2015 dollars the equivalent would be approximately $1,282.00 to $3,850.00 for each story. During a time when women did not have many opportunities for employment outside the home, Yda appreciated her financial independence and the prestige she earned as a writer.

To resolve the "Downey" issue expediently and intelligently she left San Francisco on assignment for *The Argonaut*. Pixley had contacts in Mexico City. She was to go there to investigate Mexican culture, and to write stories about her experiences abroad.

When she arrived to the country's capital, she was welcomed as an American celebrity *muy cotizada* or greatly esteemed. High-society women invited her into their homes for social occasions and literary readings. She enjoyed her popularity and resided in the home of a prominent widow.

Late one night when the wind was blustering wildly outside her window; through the gusts Yda believed she heard the sounds of a woman woefully moaning. Immediately she informed her hostess that somewhere on the street she heard a female's cry of distress.

Her patroness explained that what she heard was no mortal woman. Intrigued, the young authoress pressed for more information. Although somewhat reluctant to recount the salacious story of *La Llorona* to her young guest, nevertheless, the widow took Yda into her confidence. It was then during a windy night in Mexico City that Yda learned the fate of a maiden who ran away with and co-habituated with her inamorato.

The narration exposed the unrestrained sexual desires of two unmarried person. What happened between them, and to them, the turns and surprises were shocking. Yda had written stories about scorned women who had killed their unfaithful lovers. However, *La Llorona* told an even darker tale.

While the Church most likely created the story to scare women into obedience to religious doctrines regarding sexual relationships. On the other hand, why did Yda bring the gruesomely sensational story to Frank Pixley for publication in his *The Argonaut?*

Although Pixley founded the literary magazine as a vehicle to uncover and to fight the corruption of the San Francisco political machines, he assured his readers:

Introduction

> There is one journalistic affectation that we shall avoid, and that is, that a newspaper is governed by higher, or purer, or better motives than governed honorable men in any other relations of life. ... A newspaper is printed to make money. *The Argonaut,* April 1877.

Never ashamed of creating wealth, when Pixley founded *The Argonaut* he intended to earn a profit and he did. A decade after the California Gold Rush, there were more than 132 San Francisco newspapers and literary journals; the city was booming as the center of Western American Literature. However, by 1888 the competition between publications had dwindled down to 12 daily newspapers and 4 weekly journals.

Pixley was not a career newspaper man; instead he was an attorney by trade who enjoyed writing. Born in New York to a well positioned society family, he came west during the Gold Rush of 1848. When he started to mine for gold, he looked around and decided that there was a greater profit in defending mining claims.

He left the mines and went to San Francisco to set up a law office. The legal titles of a great deal of the land around the city were in conflict with the former Mexican government and the new California State government. The old Spanish land grants that could be proven had priority over United States land claims. However, to prove a land grant in an American court took a good deal of time and money. In the end often the land owners won, but the court costs and the attorney fees were so expensive, if the owner could not pay, the attorney took the property for payment.

As a practicing attorney, in time he developed into an excellent orator. With this aptitude he worked his way into politics. In 1858 even though the majority of his constituents were Democrats, he was elected as a Republican to represent San Francisco in the state assembly. Later on in the elections of 1861, Leland Stanford was voted in as the governor of California and Frank Pixley was elected as the state's eighth attorney general. Two years later when their terms were coming to an end in 1863, both believed that they would be nominated for reelection. However, with a split within the Republican Party, they failed to win the renomination.

After Pixley completed his term of attorney general, he traveled to Washington D.C. as a war correspondent. Although, he could not obtain a pass from Secretary of War Edwin Stanton, resourcefully Pixley visited his Democratic political rival the United States Senator from California, John Conness. He convinced the Senator to let him use his congressional pass. With that he was able to spend three months in Civil War combat areas, and at one time riding his horse to the front line with the Second Connecticut Regiment. Later he visited General Grant in his headquarters. The General commented that Pixley had seen more warfare than many of his fighting men.

After returning to San Francisco, Pixley devoted a good deal of his time to ongoing battles with his political rivals. He believed that both the Republican and the Democratic parties were run by men of suspicious character. He founded *The Argonaut* as his personal political hammer. With a large readership, in each issue he shined a bright light upon the underbellies of those who grew rich plundering taxpayer's money. When Yda sent Pixley the *La Llorona*, he had no reservations about the intent of the story; it showed the repercussion when one becomes corrupted. Upon that moral lesson, he published the story

While *The Argonaut* was successful both financially and with the reading public, Pixley continued to pursue a number of personal business interest. One of which was the railroad.

Building the railroad from the eastern part of the United Stated to the west was a huge money making project for the well-connected and enterprising capitalists known as the Big Four: Collis Huntington, Charles Crocker, Mark Hopkins, and

Leland Stanford. The ex-California governor served as president of the Southern Pacific and he was a political crony and close friend of Frank Pixley. When a land developer in San Diego, A. E. Horton, wanted a line built from San Francisco to San Diego, Pixley went to Washington acting very much like a lobbyist for the railroad. He advised Horton to make certain choice California land parcels available at a bargain price for a particular influential Congressman. In that way Pixley could insure support for the proposed railroad line. However, no evidence exists where Pixley was on the Southern Pacific's payroll; nevertheless he indeed had an intense interest in the railroad business.

The clear proof that he received direct benefit from his association with the Southern Pacific vis-à-vis Leland Stanford was with the town that was named for him. Pixley, California began as a real-estate speculation in Tulare County by two investors Darwin Allen and William Bradbury. They knew the project would be successful only if the area was connected to the main Southern Pacific line. Their solution was to invite Frank Pixley into the deal. Not only did the investors name the town in his honor, but after the railroad came to Pixley, the Southern Pacific ran ads in newspapers throughout the country, including Pixley's *The Argonaut*. The advertisements offered inexpensive train tickets to Pixley for speculation to purchasing land in and around the town. The investors offered financing for potential buyers with 25% down, the rest payable in three years at 8% interest. As a result of Frank Pixley's connection with Leland Stanford, the Pixley, Allen and Bradbury partnership enjoyed a great deal of prosperity.

Frank Pixley became a wealthy and an influential man. Owning and editing a newspaper aided his status and stature. Newspapers at the time were the most important means of communication. People relied on them for accurate reporting and those associated with the newspapers were highly regarded. *The Argonaut* provided a political podium for Pixley that led to associations with powerful individuals. From his cadre of "friends" he became a founder and a charter member of the board of directors of the San Francisco Stock Exchange in 1871, and three years later he joined a group of investors to establish the Bank of San Francisco. He also was a founding member and on the Board of Directors of The State Investment and Insurance Company, where his friend Governor Downey held a seat.

Although Pixley was involved in numerous businesses, until the day he died, he never closed his law office; instead he hired or took on partners to manage the law business.

When he founded *The Argonaut* his first editor and co-founder was Frederic Somers. Half the age of Pixley, but he was experienced in the newspaper business.

Above: Frederic Somers

The men met during the time Somers was the editorial writer and legislative correspondent for the *San Francisco Chronicle*. It was he who conceived of the idea of a weekly newspaper and invited Pixley to join him. While Somers was strong, creative and impatient, it was Pixley who provided the financial stability, and focus upon the editorial policy and the political commentary.

One of the first writers to join the new periodical's staff was Ambrose Bierce. Fiercely political, and liberal, he was a merciless critic of anyone who fell under his penetrating pen. He assured the readers,

> It is our intention to purify journalism in this town by instructing such writers as it is worthwhile to instruct and assassinating those that it is not.

He kept his promise. With his signature caustic satirical style he flayed-open those who he believed a hypocrite. He often ridiculed the Southern Pacific railroad and his employer's good friend Leland Stanford. Bierce's column entitled *Prattle* appeared at the top of column one on the front page.

Pixley, a conservative, usually opposed to Bierce's way of thinking wrote the *Olla Podrida* articles. He named his column after the Spanish dish that consisted of a boiled mish-mash of meat, fish, poultry and vegetables; it seemed an appropriate metaphor for his incongruent, but lyrical subjects that he penned about San Francisco and its environments, its present, and its future. *Olla Podrida* was placed at the top of column four also on the front page.

Frederic Somers was responsible for the insertion of the two strongly opposing view points on the front page. The Bierce and Pixley combination developed a mighty duel that kept the San Francisco readers' attention.

After about a year working for *The Argonaut* Bierce came down with "gold fever." He left San Francisco for the Black Hills of the Dakotas. Three months later he decided mining was not suited to his character. He wrote that he was returning to San Francisco, and planned to resume his work at *The Argonaut*. Pixley was not eager for his return, and Somers concurred that Bierce was dispensable. When he was not rehired, Bierce believed it was Pixley who was responsible for the insult and he never forgave him.

One of the reasons for *The Argonaut's* success was Pixley liked to add a little sugar to his political medicine. He encouraged local writers to submit poetry, prose and stories. In this way he motivated readers' interest who might not care to read about political affairs. When Pixley discovered Yda Addis she quickly became one of *The Argonaut's* most popular writers.

Yda' stories had themes of intrigue, Gothic fantasy, horror and romanticism, heroines who bravely encountered ghosts, and who possessed supernatural powers. Her female protagonists moved beyond the mid-Victorian notions of feminine passivity. These topics were on the cutting edge for her era. Even though she was a demur young lady who comported herself with dignity, if offended in someway, she

Introduction

would not speak out. The societal norms of the age shunned the passionate and independent woman.

Through her literature she questioned why women must comport themselves with docility while men, when slighted, were expected to act out; to defend their honor, if taken to the extreme ... to kill in order to maintain their reputation.

Whereas society permitted a man to act upon his wrath, women, on the other hand, were expected not to take action, instead merely to look down, fold their hands, and be quite. There were several different rules for women than for men. For instance one that stands out was women were not allowed to own real-estate, if real-property came to a female by way of an inheritance, her closest male relative was to stand in her stead. The underlying theme for women was not to speak out, not to question, merely to accept.

Although physically imprisoned by society's rules for female etiquette, Yda's mind was free from the cultural manacles. But, how was it that she began to write about liberated females; to question, and to perceive another type of decorum for women?

Most likely it was during a time in her girlhood when she lived at Fort Leavenworth, Kansas. Her father, Alfred Shea Addis, was a business savvy individual who seemed to perceive future trends. He was a Deguereotype artists by trade who brought his family to Leavenworth when the Free Staters and Confederate sympathizers were disgruntled at the Kansas – Nebraska Act. With skirmishes, bloody raids, and fights growing between the two groups, the U.S. military was forced to increase the number troops stationed at Leavenworth. The town was situated on the Western frontier where tradesmen, trappers, hunters, and people of various stripes passed through.

There were not a great many hotels where travelers could stay. Alfred bought a rooming house. He moved his family into the backrooms, had his artist gallery in the front parlor, and rented out the upstairs rooms.

When the Union Theater was offered for sale, Alfred knew that there were two other theaters in town, he perceived with the U.S. military increasing the number of troops stationed at Leavenworth, there would be a need for more entertainment. To out do his competitors who were accustomed to presenting local talent, Alfred went east to bring back seasoned performers. To no other person can be accredited with the introduction of the "star system" in Leavenwoth; with that he redefined frontier entertainment. Of course, the entertainers stayed at Alfred's boardinghouse.

Introduction

Unlike other children, Yda saw actors and actresses daily at the boardinghouse dining room, and later rehearsing, and performing. Popular stage dramas were presented at the Union Theater. There was no elaborate staging, nor costuming; the performances were similar to recitals. A different play each night, it was English literature in dramatized versions that was presented. For example Dickens' *Cricket on the Hearth*, *Chimney Corner*, and *Oliver Twist* were shown, as well as Tennyson's *Dora*; and Scott's *The Bride of Lammermoor*, *Rob Roy*, and *The Lady of the Lake*.

Yda had the unique childhood opportunity of watching some of Shakespeare's plays such as *Taming of the Shrew*, *The Merchant of Venice*, *Richard III*, *Othello*, and *Macbeth*. The barb of Avon's dramatic personification of the female, perhaps for Yda, captured the real essence of femininity. Females were portrayed as attractive, and original; often they created the main conflict or the base of the play, or they questioned the moral and cultural norms, these beautiful, strong willed women when confronting discord did not fold their hands and keep quite. Often they surpassed the male heroes. What Yda saw on stage most likely influenced her perception of relationships between men and women.

But, the town also had an impact upon her young mind. Fort Leavenworth was the busiest city on the American frontier during the most conflicting era of American history, the ramping up of the Civil War. There were all sorts of people that passed through the town. From traveling salesmen to Abolitionists, from pioneers to entertainers, the town was alive.

Although Yda was born in Lawrence, Kansas, in the winter of 1857, however after William Quantrill's bloody retaliation against the Abolitionist who had caused the deaths of some females aiding to the Confederate campaign, the atmosphere for Southern sympathizers in Lawrence was not conducive to a long life. In 1862 the Addis family moved to the safety of Leavenworth. But, not for long, two years later, when Alfred presented a benefit at the Union Theater for the victims of Quantrill's raid, it was then that the Abolitionists discovered Alfred was a pro-slaver who owned the most popular theater in town. They torched his establishment. Not only did the theater burn down but the entire city block was left in ashes.

By covered wagon the Addis family and their slave moved to Northern Mexico. There many Confederate sympathizers found refuge. To earn a living, Alfred photographed the landscape and the indigenous people using the Ambrotype and Ferrotype methods. He'd send his photographs to his agent in New York.

Introduction

Above: Alfred Shea Addis

Above: Photo made by Alfred Shea Addis. He was a prolific photographer; however, there are but a handful of his photographs that have survived.

Yda often accompanied her father on his photographic expeditions. She learned the Spanish language and some of the indigenous dialects in order to converse with and to encourage the native people to sit for her father's camera. As Alfred searched for different scenery and environments for his photography, gradually the family transmigrated to the western coastal port of Mazatlan, Mexico.

After the Civil War, the Addis family returned to the United States aboard the *SS Orizaba*. The 1,400 ton steamship ran cargo and the U.S. Mail from San Francisco, California, to the Isthmus of Panama. A difficult run, but the narrow boat had two masts, and a paddlewheel. With that equipment, Captain Henry James Johnson could maneuver her through rough seas.

The Captain was originally from Massachusetts where he and his brother owned a whaling ship; they were forced to close down their business when the Army Corps of Engineers reported that the Boston waters were being over whaled. Henry James moved to California and began working for the Pacific Mail Company that owned numerous ships including the *SS Orizaba*. His experience with violent waters as a whaler was an asset when he brought the ship into the port of Wilmington, California. Later, in 1883, Yda wrote an article for *The Weekly Pomona Times* that described her 1873 voyage from Mazatlan, Mexico, to Los Angeles, California. In the March 17th article she wrote "The sea was so rough that the

Introduction

narrow steamer pitched almost beyond the possibility of debarking, but, then as some of the sea-wise said, 'The *Orizaba* would roll in a mill race.'"

Yda was thirteen years old when she arrived to Los Angeles, California. After living in Mexico, she was more familiar with the Spanish language than the English. She enrolled in the Los Angeles public school and afterwards earned high marks. Upon graduating in 1875, she began to teach school in Tustin, California.

Above: The *SS Orizaba* had sails, a steam engine, and a paddle wheel. With that set-up she could get herself out of the most extreme difficulties. The Pacific Mail Company had the U.S. Mail contract from San Francisco, California to the Isthmus of Panama, and the ports in between.

When Pixley decided to publish her first story in the May 22nd 1880 issue of *The Argonaut*, it changed her life. His readership approved of her work and requested more. On a regular basis Pixley began to feature Yda's stories in his journal. Gradually she gained fame as a writer. She quit teaching school, moved to San Francisco with her mother Sarah, and became a professional author. By the time *La Llorona* appeared in the March 10, 1888 edition of Pixley's journal, Yda was famous.

Pixley had championed the idea that women should be able to work outside the home in professions other than teachers, laundresses, nurses, and maids. In 1869 during a speech he gave to the Masons he said "even the ladies, God bless them, are striking for higher privileges and clamoring for their just rights. If they attain a higher power, or have the right to exercise any greater authority than they now wield, I desire to be understood that I was always for them." His belief in women authoresses was a matter of record. He judged literature on writing ability alone, one-third of the writers of *The Argonaut* were women.

When Yda sent the story of *La Llorona* to Pixley, he published it the week before Good Friday, of the Easter season. Most likely through Yda's literary efforts Pixley was sermonizing to his political enemies, showing them what can happen if one steps away from decency and falls from grace into chicanery and corruption.

Introduction

While the Church most likely employed the horrific tale of *La Llorona* as a teaching tool, so did Frank Pixley. The ending of the story provided no redemption for the maiden's fall from grace and likewise for her aristocratic lover's deception. For eternity on dark windy nights the ghost of La Llorona haunts the streets of Mexico City; on the morning after she appears the flowers on her lover's tomb become "withered, seared, and the earth upon it dank and putrid, as if it were drenched and soaked with blood."

The wicked legend of *La Llorona* was retold for centuries in private parlors, around late night campfires, and in dark corners. The story never appeared in any publication until 1888 when Yda Addis sent it to her publisher in San Francisco.

Of course, Ambrose Bierce fiercely opposed Pixley's type of social sermons. He thought of him as a phony prevaricator. Upon Pixley's death on August 13, 1895, Bierce's nature couldn't pass up the opportunity to criticize his former employer one more time when he wrote:

Here lies Frank Pixley ...as usual.

La Llorona

The Wailing Woman
An Ancient Legend of Mexico.

by

Yda Addis

It was three o'clock in the morning. The bells of the cathedral and the palace, far away, struck the hour, as we traversed a lonely, silent street toward the suburbs of Mexico City. We had been keeping vigil with a wounded man, a compatriot of mine, and had overstayed our watch, for he was frantic with delirium, and we feared to transfer him to the care of the inexperienced and rather careless persons who should succeed us.

We walked on briskly; for it was long hours past the time when coaches and tram-cars were running. We were in

San Cosme, and in front of the great, massive structure which the wife of ex-Marshal Bazaine has claimed from the government as an imperial gift to her traitorous husband. The facade of this building curves in such fashion as to form an offset or alcove on the street, and before we reached it I thought I saw a woman's figure stealing along in its denser shadow, and I felt a thrill of compassion for her, as one of the poor children of the night. She was not to be seen when we came near the spot, but a moment later a piercing cry rang out near us -- a long drawn wail of suffering and horror.

I grasped the arm of my companion. "Some woman is in distress -- we must go to her rescue. We are both armed, more than heaven!"

But he threw his arm about me, and forced me forward at a quick pace that was almost a run; and so unexpected was his behavior that I could not resist.

"Come on! Come on!" he whispered hoarsely, as I shook myself free from his clasp, "we must hurry! We must go on quickly!"

"I would not have believed you could desert a fellow creature in trouble!" I said with indignation, "and beyond all, a woman. It is not like you, Federico." Because I had seen his courage tried by venomous serpents in tierra caliente; and in encounters with highwaymen in the Sierras; and I had heard of his coolness and daring in a combat with Apaches in Northern Chihuahua.

"Hush! Hush!" he answered, panting. "You do not know what you are saying. We did not leave a mortal woman -- the voice you hear is the cry of La Llorona. Look over there at the sentinel!"

We were near one of the points where a watchman stands all night in the middle of the thoroughfare, and following my companion's gestures, I saw the officer, fallen upon his knees in the circle of light cast by his lantern; the great capuchin hood of his cape was pulled over his head, and every line of his figure betokened abject fear and horror. There was something uncanny in the sight, for the policemen of Mexico are not impressionable material. And through the silent, empty street those dreadful cries still went ringing wildly, surely sufficient motive for such a display of terror. The sound seemed to float away, and down a by-street toward the equestrian statue of Charles IV, growing fainter and fainter in the distance.

"Let's go," said my companion; "yes, I am skeptic, and I sneer at spiritualism, and ghosts, and phantoms; but, nevertheless, I think there is not a man or woman in Mexico who would not tremble at the voice of Luisa La Llorona."

****

In the year 1584, Luisa Haro was known as the most beautiful girl in Mexico, and the most unpresumptuous. Her father had brought her from Spain when she was ten years old, and, he had died four years later, had left her without family, so far it was known. She was a clever needle-woman, and a maker of artificial silk flowers, and her skill found ready employment for churchly uses, notwithstanding the enormous quantity of such work done in the convents. Her little home was located in a lovely callejuela, or bystreet, almost like an alley, in the shadow of the cloister-walls of one of the guilds that chiefly employed her, and here she lived, forlornly enough, indeed, as is the fate of a woman who dwells quite alone; but her days were virtuous and tranquil. It did not matter to her when the gallants came stealing at nightfall into that rincón apartado -- that out-of-the-way corner, and occupied the narrow passage in the dusty midnight darkness. Her shuttered widows and doors were closed and barred at sunset; and none of the delicate, scented fingers that tapped on those clumsy defenses ever sounded the "Open Sesame!" to the girl they sheltered. Luisa was the despair of all the happy, dissolute blades of the vice-regal court of New Spain. Her neighbors in the lonely alley had mixed feeling about the girl, uncertain whether to respect and commend her severe integrity or to disparage her, as one who is denied the natural passions and pleasant frailties of humanity.

But a change came about when the girl was about twenty years old. The gossips of the neighborhood began to whisper that the shutters of Luisa's window now creaked slightly open, and that her voice was heard at the crevice in converse with one who came not tentatively and doubting, but with the confident, assured step of a man who knows the welcome that awaits him. And soon it was told about, originating in one of the vague, indefinite ways in which such things do transpire, that this complacent wooer was Nuño, Marquis of Montes-Claros. So it was that Luisa assumed a new importance in the eyes of those about her, as what happens under like conditions.

One night -- a night when the dashing rain scourged the black walls of the cloister, to the mournful accompaniment of the moaning owls in the belfry -- one of the parish good men was hurrying home through the narrow alley where Luisa lived, when he saw before him something that made him pause and tremble. He was of the timid bourgeois class that carried no weapon, no knife, nor slender deadly rapier swung from his belt.

The night was dark, almost to palpability. No ray of light fell into the alley, except the dim ray from the little lantern, swinging before the rude image of some saint in a niche near the tablet on the wall, at the entrance of the alley where it opened with a blunt angle into a wider thoroughfare. That ray, falling through the weather-stained pane of the lantern, was dim and fitful, and almost seemed to make the darkness denser, and more concrete than the shapes that the honest wayfarer thought he saw flitting along the wall. Now these might be some of the gallants that were always wrangling hereabouts for the sweet sake of Luisa, albeit there had been a notable falling-off in their attendance, since it was rumored she had finally hearkened to the voice of one of their number. Or -- and the hair of the honest fellow bristled at the idea-- it might even be Don Nuño himself, and his worship, by all accounts, would not hesitate to spit like a curlew from the marshes on one whom he might meet poaching on his woman. So, fearing to be mistaken for a gallant, the honest citizen shrunk into himself, and flattened his portliness against the convent wall as best might be. And the vague shapes passed him by in silence, unperceiving.

He repented timidity the next morning, and reviled himself for a fool and a coward, when the neighborhood thrilled to the news of the flight of Luisa Haro. Her door stood ajar, and her poor belongings were left undisturbed. All the evidence pointed to the fact that her flight was voluntary and deliberate, and the popular theory was unanimous in declaring that her comrade must be Nuño, Marquis of Montes-Claros. It was this couple, no doubt, whom the good man had seen stealing away through the darkness, and his repentance was keen that he had not followed them, to possess himself of that knowledge of their movements and destination that would have made him important among his fellows.

From that day, her old-time neighbors knew nothing of Luisa Haro, except that some one whose affairs had taken him to the suburb of San Cosme brought back the story that he had seen her there, blooming and with sumptuous accessories, in the balcony of a splendid mansion that was known to belong to Montes-Claros.

****

Six years after Luisa left from her home in the narrow alley, she sat in the luxurious home where Montes-Claros had placed her, brooding mournfully over her situation. The moonlight streamed through the open window and illuminated her despondent figure. In the face and form she was more beautiful than on the day she fled with Montes-Claros, but still was she not beautiful enough to keep the fickle fancy of the Spaniard. His attentions and his interest had gradually diminished, until the unhappy woman now had but too much reason to consider herself altogether deserted by him for whom she had given up all that is most dear to woman. She lacked no material comfort, it is true, thus far, but this was little consolation to a woman whose thwarted affection was as strong and unaltered as when her passionate heart first poured out its ardent incense before her lover.

She had not seen Montes-Claros for a fortnight, and she was resolved to know the worst without further horror of suspense and anxiety. She got up, and carried the infant in her arms to an alcove, behind whose silken curtains lay two older children sleeping. She laid the little one beside its brothers. She put on a long, dark, clinging cloak, left the house, and made her way to the central streets of the city.

She knew the family mansion of Montes-Claros, and shortly found herself before it. The windows of the facade were ablaze with light, and she saw that the rooms were full of a festive crowd. Nuño was there in the midst of his guests with his proud, affected mother, and beside them a young girl, tall and handsome, wearing a bridal gown.

Then Luisa's heart sank like lead. She pulled the sleeve a bystander, gazing like herself through the window. "Do you know, friend, who is the young lady beside the Señor Marquis?"

"Who should it be," laughed the man she questioned, "but his novia -- the bride he married this morning at ten o'clock in the chapel of the Sagrario?"

Luisa could not speak, but neither did she cry out, only stepped back from the window, and pushed her way to the open street through the eager crowd of on-lookers.

Slowly, mechanically she found her way, never rushing, never pausing, till she reached the house in San Cosme, and let herself in at its great arched entrance, and into her own bedroom. An antique coffer stood there, an ancient cedar chest with Moresque decoration, brought from Spain by the family of Montes-Claros. In it Nuño kept, while he yet frequented the home, such odds and ends that he didn't need immediately at the time, or things at the moment that he found cumbrous.

Still under the spell of that awful, deadly quiet, Luisa opened the old chest, and took from it a dagger, a curious jeweled weapon, that Nuño had tossed in it long months since, and forgotten, though its memory had lived in the fevered brain of the woman.

Still lit only by the pallid, ghastly moonbeams, she went to the alcove where her little ones lay sleeping, and drew aside the curtains.

"Your father has forsaken us, my darling ones, and your mother wants to protect you from the miseries that await you. To God I recommend your innocent spirits."

Then, one by one, slowly, surely, fatally, she thrust the dagger into the bosom of each tender little body.

Only when the blood welled darkly up, staining the white night clothes, did the wretched mother seem to realize her dreadful doing. She gazed a moment at the heart-rending vision, and then ran forth into the streets, uttering those frightful wails that for three hundred years have continued to echo in the streets of Mexico City at varying hours and seasons -- when the soul in penance can no longer endure its torture, so the devout say.

As the wailing woman ran that night, her cries aroused the city, and she was captured and recognized, when the dagger she still clutched, and her blood-stained clothes, told the tragic story, and gave the clue to discovery of her victims. There was no penalty for man's inhumanity to woman in Mexico of those days, any more than in the present; and the poor distracted instrument of crime paid the temporal penalty in this case, while the actual murderer, in fact, rather gained popularity.

During her imprisonment and trial, Luisa maintained a helpless, hopeless silence. She failed and faded day by day, and when, at last, arrived the hour of execution, she was unable to walk up the steps of the scaffold, and, not from fright, but sheer weakness, she became senseless in the arms of her bearers. The execution proceeded, but the decree of the law was done on a corpse because the noose never touched her, Luisa Haro was lifeless.

And, however justice had miscarried in the hands of human authority, the retribution of heaven proved direct and active. For, on that very May day when the woman who had trusted him went to the doom of a felon, Nuño Marquis de Montes-Claros, was buried, having died before his honeymoon was over.

And now, centuries after, it is told that, whenever appears the Wailing Woman, the following morning sees the flowers on the tomb of Montes-Claros withered, seared, and the earth upon it dank and putrid, as if it were drenched and soaked with blood.

Yda Addis.
Mexico City, March, 1888.

The Front Cover

Nancy Glenn-Nieto created the image on the front cover. While Yda Addis used words to generate mental descriptions of the *La Llorona*, it was Nancy who turned words into a pictorial representation of the tormented protagonist of the ancient Mexican legend.

Nancy, not unlike Yda Addis, was born in the United States, and later spent a good deal of her life in Mexico. Both author and painter-- lovely ladies, kind and generous to their friends and family, however, the horrific expression on the face of Nancy's *La Llorona* along with the bloody knife raised aggressively as if in a crazed disbelief of what she had done, was shocking. So much so I had to ask Nancy how did she come up with this image of *La Llorona*?

Her answer, "It was a combination of Yda Addis' description of *La Llorona*, and from my experiences of the Day of the Dead when I lived in Mexico."

***

Nancy began painting when she was a girl. According to her mother, she'd often bring home stray little dogs and cats. She'd paint their portraits, and then adopted the little critters to become part of her family.

During her high school days, her first paid job as an artist was painting a Christmas scene on the front windows of a local business in her hometown. Later, after she graduated from the University of California, Santa Barbara, with a degree in fine-art, she moved to Mexico City, with the hope to begin a career as a fine-arts painter.

Mexico always had an affinity for her. She learned about the country from her grandmother Herminia Harrell, who was born in Chihuahua, Mexico, and with her family had escaped the Mexican Revolution of 1911, into the safety of Texas.

When Nancy moved to Mexico City, she often visited art galleries where she had the opportunities to met artists such as Francisco Toledo, Rufino Tamayo, and David Alfaro Siqueiros. The latter had invited her to the opening of Siqueiros' new "Poly-forum." That was where she met her future husband the internationally renowned painter Rodolfo Nieto.

He had recently returned to Mexico after ten years living and working in Paris. Handsomely tall, with a shock of dark wavy hair, and cat-like green eyes, he impressed Nancy; their courtship lasted a few months when on September 11, 1971, they married at the Civil Register in Coyoacan, Mexico.

Their home in Tacubaya, Mexico, was large and well appointed. The walls were painted a dark peach color; in the living room Rodolfo installed a sizeable turquoise throw-rug and in the adjoining dining room he laid down a bright tangerine toned carpet. Rodolfo's paintings adorned the walls and Nancy's Mexican Masks collection hung on the walls of the stairway to the bedrooms.

Towards the back of the home on the ground floor, they had arranged a studio where they spent a great deal of time painting. He, with his vibrant large canvases, was continually preparing for his next gallery show; she learned from Rodolfo how difficult it was to prepare an exhibition. Themes, colors, canvass sizes -- all of these things had to work together for a successful presentation.

In 1983, Rodolfo encouraged Nancy to step forward to create her own show. Upon her debut, the critics and the public accepted her work with a good deal of favor.

Since then she continues to have shows. As a successful artist, her art work hangs in many distinguished museums and private collections.

www.ingramcontent.com/pod-product-compliance
Lightning Source LLC
Chambersburg PA
CBHW061310040426
42444CB00010B/2574